ESSENTIAL POEMS
FOR CHILDREN

ESSENTIAL POEMS FOR CHILDREN

(First Aid for Frantic Parents)

EDITED BY
DAISY GOODWIN

HarperCollins*Publishers*

HarperCollins*Publishers*
77–85 Fulham Palace Road,
Hammersmith, London w6 8jb
www.harpercollins.co.uk

Published by HarperCollins*Publishers* 2005

10 9 8 7 6 5 4 3 2 1

A catalogue record for this book
is available from the British Library

ISBN 0 00 720208 3

Set in PostScript Linotype Minion with Optima display
Typeset by Rowland Phototypesetting Ltd, Bury St Edmunds, Suffolk

Printed and bound in Great Britain by Clays Ltd, St Ives plc

Visit www.AuthorTracker.co.uk for exclusive information
on your favourite HarperCollins authors

CONTENTS

INTRODUCTION

One of my earliest childhood memories is of leaning on my grand-mother's shoulder as she recited the opening lines of 'Horatio at the Bridge' by Lord Macauley,

> Lars Porsena of Clusium
> By the Nine Gods he swore
> That the great house of Tarquin
> Should suffer wrong no more.
> By the Nine Gods he swore it,
> And named a trysting day,
> And bade his messengers ride forth,
> East and west and south and north,
> To summon his array.

I can't have been more than four or five, with only the dimmest idea of who Lars Porsena was and why Horatio was standing on the bridge, but I understood enough to know that one was good and one was bad. What I knew for sure was that my grandmother smelt of Yardley's Lavender and that while she was reading this poem, no harm could come to me. I would lie with my head on her thin chest and feel it vibrate as she delivered Macauley's lines with all the gusto of her Edwardian childhood. Her father had read the same poems to her, her two sisters and her beloved brother Walter. I now think the little catch in her voice as she came to Horatio's heroic last stand had everything to do with Walter, who received a posthumous award for gallantry at the Somme. That poem is a ribbon tying one generation of my family to another. When I read 'Horatio' to my youngest daughter and I feel the weight of her head on my chest and listen to the way her breathing begins to slow in response to the steady pulse of that imperial metre, I wonder if she can sense in my voice the love I felt for my long dead, much-missed grandmother.

I have been lucky that the legacy of poetry that my grandmother left me was so rich. For me, poetry is a dressing up box to be played with, not an exam tinged cupboard under the stairs to be avoided at all costs. To read poetry to your children not only exposes them to great art, but it creates a magical bond between you. When I was researching this book, I asked a group of nine year olds at my daughter's school to recommend their favourite poems (many of which I have included here). Nearly all of them connected their favourite poem to a mother, father, or grandmother, who had lodged those lines in their emotional hard drive for ever. I love the idea of poems as precious heirlooms passed down from generation to generation. This book is designed for parents to read to their children at the end of a long, hard day, so that both parties can leave the world behind.

Reading poetry aloud is an intimate, transforming process; the secret reverberations of rhythm travel further than any prose. Children, especially those who can't read yet, adore strongly rhyming verse – I think they like the way that rhyme gives them a sense of control over the words they can't yet decipher. Poetry can be practical too; I always read poems to my boisterous four year old at bedtime because I find that poetry is about the only thing that will lull her into a state where sleep is an option. Not to mention the fact that ten poems area darn sight easier to read that the tedious doings of Maisie, Spot and Angelina Ballerina. Such is the invisible support afforded by metre, that even the most exhausted parent can give an award-winning performance when reading poetry. Exaggerate like mad and let yourself go! The therapeutic effect extends in both directions, I find that after an intensive poetry session my craving for the evening glass of white wine diminishes.

This is not a comprehensive anthology; I wanted to create a book that would fit in small hands. Some of the poems are famous, some are not; but all come with a child's recommendation. I have grouped the poems very loosely into the categories that affect all children – family, food, school, appearance, fairies ... My suggestion is to open the book at random and see what happens – but if your audience is particularly tired and fractious, head for the bedtime section and concentrate on the Robert Louis Stevenson poems.

I hope that you and your children enjoy this book. For small children, poetry is a joy, because poets, like children, are discovering the world anew, every single day. I don't know if anyone has studied the effects of reading poetry to children on their subsequent development, but I am convinced that getting your children into the habit of reading poetry is like handing them the key to a secret garden. Learning your times tables is important but realising that in your head anything is possible is the most precious gift of all.

An indecent number of people have helped me to compile this book. First and foremost is my sister Tabitha Potts without whom this book would not exist. A huge thank you too to the incomparable Andrea Bartlett and the Class of 2006 at Bute House who furnished me with a selection of their favourite poems and shared with me their witty, perceptive and heartfelt perceptions about poetry.

I must also thank Aviva Halter-Hurn for her glorious illustrations, Connie Robertson for her ruthless pursuit of copyright and my daughters Lydia and Ottie for doing all the market research for this book. Thanks too to my old editor Mike Fishwick and my new editor Clare Reihill and to Kate Hyde for keeping everything together.

ESSENTIAL POEMS
FOR CHILDREN

A POETICAL MENAGERIE

I make no apology for the size of this poetical menagerie:
so many children love and respond to animals that I believe
an appreciation of animals' beauty and strength is
hardwired into the human brain. If you don't agree with
me, take a look at the animal cave paintings discovered in
France, or read the stories of the Aboriginal Dream Time,
or the African fables of Anansi the Spider. My daughter
Ottilie became a vegetarian from the age of seven onwards
(to a certain amount of consternation from the family
cook, myself) and loves all animals passionately with the
possible exception of pigeons.

And, of course, a love of animals is not confined to
children. Here we have poets from W. B. Yeats to Ted
Hughes celebrating the humble squirrel or the bizarre and
otherworldly jellyfish. The animals most present in
children's lives – pets – get a good mention here, such as
Karla Kuskin's charming 'You Are the Kind of Dog I Love'.
I've also included 'To a Monkey' by the nineteenth-century
child prodigy Marjory Fleming, as an example of the
marvellous poems children write themselves.

A lot of the children who contributed poems mentioned
that this was also their mother or father's favourite: an
inspiring example of how a poem can give pleasure for

generation after generation. I've also included Spike Milligan's wonderful 'The Squirdle' and 'Magic Cat' by Peter Dixon, as all children love fantasy and imaginary beasts (and adults too, read *The Book of Imaginary Beings* by Jorge Luis Borges and Margarita Guerro for a wonderful collection of mythical animals). It is the fun, wordplay and enjoyment of the imagination in these poems which have, above all, been the reason why I chose them.

Children also love to be frightened (a bit!) and for that reason I have included poems on several scary carnivores, such as the shark in Jack Prelutsky's poem. They also love to marvel at the large (such as Ogden Nash's elephant) and the small (so A. A. Milne's poem about Alexander the Beetle, 'Forgiven', has found a place here). Again, the ant and the flea and other creepy crawlies are very interesting to children, who don't necessarily possess the adult 'yuck' reaction to insects, so I've included a few poems about the less attractive beasts in the world. It can all be summed up by William Blake's 'Three Things to Remember' and Christina Rossetti's 'Hurt No Living Thing' as we all hope our children will do a better job of looking after the world's creatures than our generation has managed to do.

To a Squirrel at Kyle-na-no

Come play with me;
Why should you run
Through the shaking tree
As though I'd a gun
To strike you dead?
When all I would do
Is to scratch your head
And let you go.

W. B. Yeats

Answer to a Child's Question

Do you ask what the birds say? The Sparrow, the Dove,
The Linnet and Thrush say, 'I love and I love!'
In the winter they're silent – the wind is so strong;
What it says, I don't know, but it sings a loud song.
But green leaves, and blossoms, and sunny warm weather,
And singing, and loving – all come back together.
But the Lark is so brimful of gladness and love,
The green fields below him, the blue sky above,
That he sings, and he sings; and for ever sings he –
'I love my Love, and my Love loves me!'

Samuel Taylor Coleridge

To a Monkey

O lovely O most charming pug
Thy gracefull air and heavenly mug
The beauties of his mind do shine
And every bit is shaped so fine
Your very tail is most devine
Our teeth is whiter than the snow
You are a great buck and a bow
Your eyes are of so fine a shape
More like a christains than an ape
His cheeks is like the roses blume
Your hair is like the ravens plume
His noses cast is of the roman
He is a very pretty weoman
I could not get a rhyme for roman
And was oblidged to call it weoman.

Marjory Fleming

Never Never Disagree

Never never disagree
With a shark beneath the sea,
Lest you feel a sudden crunch
And discover you are lunch.

Jack Prelutsky

Jellyfish

When my chandelier
Waltzes pulsing near
Let the swimmer fear.

Beached and bare
I'm less of a scare
But I don't care.

Though I look like a slob
It's a delicate job
Being just a blob.

Ted Hughes

You Are the Kind of Dog I Love

You are the kind of dog I love because
you are a walking hill of hair.
And even though I cannot see your
eyes
ears
nose
or paws
I somehow know
that you
are under there.

Karla Kuskin

The Squirdle

I thought I saw a Squirdle
I think I thought I saw
I think I thunk I thought
I saw a Squirdle by my door

If it was not a Squirdle
I thought I thunk I saw
Then what in heaven's name was it
That gave a Squirdle roar?

Perhaps I saw a Pussel-skwonk!
But that would be absurd
Because I think I thunk it was
A Squirdle that I heard

So if I saw a Pussel-skwonk
Yet heard a Squirdle roar
It means I think I thunk I thought
I'd seen what I had saw!

Spike Milligan

If You Should Meet a Crocodile

If you should meet a crocodile,
Don't take a stick and poke him,
Ignore the welcome in his smile,
Be careful not to stroke him.

For as he sleeps upon the Nile,
He thinner gets and thinner,
And whenever you meet a crocodile,
He's ready for his dinner!

Anonymous

Kindness to Animals

Riddle cum diddle cum dido,
My little dog's name is Fido;
I bought him a wagon,
And hitched up a dragon,
And off we both went for a ride, oh!

Riddle cum diddle cum doodle,
My little cat's name is Toodle;
I curled up her hair,
But she only said, 'There!
You've made me look just like a poodle!'

Riddle cum diddle cum dinky,
My little pig's name is Winky;
I keep him quite clean
With the washing machine,
And I rinse him all off in the sinkie.

Laura Richards

The Frog

Be kind and tender to the Frog,
And do not call him names;
As 'Slimy skin', or 'Polly-wog',
Or likewise 'Ugly James',
Or 'Gap-a-grin', or 'Toad-gone-wrong',
Or 'Billy Bandy-knees':
The Frog is justly sensitive
To epithets like these.
No animal will more repay
A treatment kind and fair;
At least so lonely people say,
Who keep a frog (and, by the way
They are extremely rare).

Hilaire Belloc

Fear Fly

If I was a fly,
I don't suppose,
I'd want to land
On someone's nose.
A nose is meant
To run or drip
And not be used as
A landing strip.
I'd never land
Upon an ear,
You never know
What you might hear,
Never land on
A sailor's belly
That's how we lost
Auntie Nelly.
The most dangerous place
To land I know
Is either Gatwick
Or Heathrow.

Spike Milligan

Swimming Teeth

I'm not a do-as-you're-told-fish,
A looked-at-in-a-bowl-fish,
A stay-still-to-behold-fish,
An as-you-can-guess, a goldfish.

Where sea is blue, I make it red
Where body bubbles, I slash, I shred,
Where eyes see light, I blur them dark,
Where skin shines bright, I expose a heart.

Humans call me shark,
But to my friends of the deep
I am known as Swimming Teeth
And one day I'd like to direct a movie.

John Agard

Forgiven

I found a little beetle, so that Beetle was his name,
And I called him Alexander and he answered just the same
I put him in a match-box, and I kept him all the day . . .
And Nanny let my beetle out –

Yes, Nanny let my beetle out –
She went and let my beetle out –
And Beetle ran away

She said she didn't mean it and I never said she did,
She said she wanted matches and she just took off the lid,
She said that she was sorry, but it's difficult to catch
An excited sort of beetle you've mistaken for a match.

She said that she was sorry, and I really mustn't mind,
As there's lots and lots of beetles which she's certain we could find,
If we looked about the garden for the holes where beetles hid –
And we'd get another match-box and write BEETLE on the lid

We went to all the places which a beetle might be near,
And we made the sort of noises which a beetle likes to hear,
And I saw a kind of something and I gave a sort of shout:
'A beetle-house and Alexander Beetle is coming out!'

It was Alexander Beetle I'm as certain as can be,
And he had a sort of look as if he thought it must be Me
And he had a sort of look as if he thought he ought to say:
'I'm very, very sorry that I tried to run away.'

And Nanny's very sorry too for you-know-what-she-did,
And she's writing Alexander very blackly on the lid.
So Nan and me are friends now because it's difficult to catch
An excited Alexander you've mistaken for a match.

A. A. Milne

My Dog Spot

I have a white dog
Whose name is Spot,
And sometimes he's white
And sometimes he's not.
But whether he's white
Or whether he's not,
There's a patch on his ear
That makes him Spot.

He has a tongue
That is long and pink,
And he lolls it out
When he wants to think.
He seems to think most
When the weather is hot
He's a wise sort of dog,
Is my dog, Spot.

He likes a bone
And he likes a ball,
But he doesn't care
For a cat at all.
He waggles his tail
And he knows what's what,
So I'm glad that he's my dog,
My dog, Spot.

Rodney Bennett

The Caterpillar

Brown and furry
Caterpillar in a hurry,
Take your walk
To the shady leaf, or stalk,
Or what not,
Which may be the chosen spot.
No toad spy you,
Hovering bird of prey pass by you;
Spin and die,
To live again a butterfly.

Christina Rossetti

The Elephant

When people call this beast to mind,
They marvel more and more
At such a little tail behind
SO LARGE a trunk before.

Hilaire Belloc

The Flea

And here's the happy, bounding flea –
You cannot tell the he from she.
The sexes look alike, you see;
But she can tell and so can he.

Roland Young

Magic Cat

My mum whilst walking through the door
Spilt some magic on the floor.
Blobs of this
and splots of that
but most of it upon the cat.

Our cat turned magic, straight away
and in the garden went to play
where it grew two massive wings
and flew around in fancy rings.
'Oh look!' cried Mother, pointing high,
'I didn't know our cat could fly.'
Then with a dash of Tibby's tail
she turned my mum into a snail!

So now she lives beneath a stone
and dusts around a different home.
And I'm an ant
and Dad's a mouse
And Tibby's living in our house.

Peter Dixon

Hurt No Living Thing

Hurt no living thing,
Ladybird nor butterfly,
Nor moth with dusty wing,
Nor cricket chirping cheerily,
Nor grasshopper, so light of leap,
Nor dancing gnat,
Nor beetle fat,
Nor harmless worms that creep.

Christina Rossetti

The Camel's Complaint

Canary-birds feed on sugar and seed,
Parrots have crackers to crunch;
And as for the poodles, they tell me the noodles
Have chicken and cream for their lunch.
But there's never a question
About *my* digestion –
Anything does for me.

Cats, you're aware, can repose in a chair,
Chickens can roost upon rails;
Puppies are able to sleep in a stable,
And oysters can slumber in pails.
But no one supposes
A poor camel dozes –
Any place does for me.

Lambs are enclosed where it's never exposed,
Coops are constructed for hens;
Kittens are treated to houses well heated.
And pigs are protected by pens.
But a camel comes handy
Wherever it's sandy –
Anywhere does for me.

People would laugh if you rode a giraffe,
Or mounted the back of an ox;
It's nobody's habit to ride on a rabbit,
Or try to bestraddle a fox.

But as for a camel, he's
Ridden by families –
Any load does for me.

A snake is as round as a hole in the ground,
And weasels are wavy and sleek;
And no alligator could ever be straighter
Than lizards that live in a creek.
But a camel's all lumpy
And bumpy and humpy –
Any shape does for me.

Charles E. Carryl

On the Ning Nang Nong

On the Ning Nang Nong
Where the Cows go Bong!
And the Monkeys all say Boo!
There's a Nong Nang Ning
Where the trees go Ping!
And the tea pots Jibber Jabber Joo.
On the Nong Ning Nang
All the mice go Clang!
And you just can't catch 'em when they do!
So it's Ning Nang Nong!
Cows go Bong!
Nong Nang Ning!
Trees go Ping!
Nong Ning Nang!
The mice go Clang!
What a noisy place to belong,
Is the Ning Nang Ning Nang Nong.

Spike Milligan

Three Things to Remember

A Robin Redbreast in a cage
Puts all Heaven in a rage.

A skylark wounded on the wing
Doth make a cherub cease to sing.

He who shall hurt the little wren
Shall never be beloved by men.

William Blake

Ants, Although Admirable, Are Awfully Aggravating

The busy ant works hard all day
And never stops to rest or play.
He carries things ten times his size,
And never grumbles, whines or cries.
And even climbing flower stalks,
He always runs, he never walks.
He loves his work, he never tires,
And never puffs, pants or perspires.

Yet though I praise his boundless vim
I am not really fond of him.

Walter R. Brooks

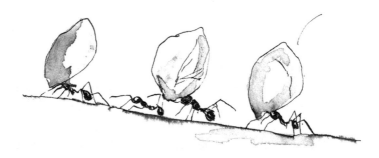

MY FAMILY AND OTHER ANIMALS

These poems reverberate with me a great deal as a parent. For example, before we had my daughter Lydia, my elder child Ottilie once wrote an illustrated essay saying 'I don't want a sister or a brother, I'm happy on my own'. 'Mum is Having a Baby' by Colin McNaughton reminds us of the seismic shock any child encounters when knocked off its perch by a new arrival. As its young contributor wrote, 'I like this poem because it reminds me of how my brother must have felt when my mother had me.'

Some of the poems focus on rules and regulations, and how it feels to be on the receiving end of that constant parental 'No'. Take Spike Milligan's 'Kids', where the child narrator asks 'If then we kids/Cause such a fuss,/Why do you go on/Having us?'. 'Top Twenty Things That Parents Never Say' will find an appreciative audience in teenagers and remind parents, perhaps, of how often we let ourselves go on auto-pilot when dealing with people not old enough to vote but old enough to have an independent opinion.

But of course the family is, one hopes, where children will have their happiest times. 'Granny Anna' by Yansan Agard is a charming poem celebrating the bond between a grandparent and their grandchild; the American poet Shel Silverstein's 'The Little Boy and the Old Man' similarly speaks of the bonds between old and young people, while Langston Hughes's 'Mother to Son' is about the wisdom we try to pass on to our kids. Hughes had an unhappy childhood himself (though he was very close to his grandmother) but this poem to me speaks of parental love of a gritty and realistic kind. Finally, 'Accident' by Gervase Phinn and 'Watch Your French' by Kit Wright are all about the silly mistakes we make when our children are (make no doubt about it) watching, and learning . . .

Top Twenty Things That Parents Never Say

- Of course you can have more pocket money.
- I bought those chocolate biscuits just for you.
- No, it won't hurt to leave your bike out in the rain.
- The telephone is free if you wish to use it.
- Don't bother with the dishes, I'll do them later.
- I do wish the school wouldn't give you so much homework.
- I like your friend with the nose stud and the tattoos.
- You're not coming in too early tonight are you?
- Just leave your dirty underwear on the floor.
- Don't worry, I came bottom of the class when I was your age.
- I hope you enjoy the rest of the late-night film.
- Would you like any help sticking that poster on your bedroom wall?
- These trainers are very cheap.
- Would you like lots of greasy food at your all-night party?
- I don't think the dog is ready for a walk yet.
- Why don't you stay in bed a little longer this morning?
- I do hate a tidy room.
- Leave all the lights on, will you?
- Don't bother cleaning out the bath.
- School holidays are a bit short this year.

Gervase Phinn

Mum is Having a Baby

Mum is having a baby!
I'm shocked! I'm all at sea!
What's she want another one for:
WHAT'S THE MATTER WITH ME?

Colin McNaughton

Kids

'Sit up straight',
Said mum to Mabel.
'Keep your elbows
Off the table.
Do not eat peas
Off a fork.
Your mouth is full –
Don't try and talk.
Keep your mouth shut
When you eat.
Keep still or you'll
Fall off your seat.
If you want more,
You will say, "please".
Don't fiddle with that piece of cheese!'
If then we kids
Cause such a fuss,
Why do you go on
Having us?

Spike Milligan

Granny Anna

I love my Granny Anna
Yes I love her so
For when I was little
She could never let me go

I care a lot about her
Like she does for me
When I'm with her I'm happy
And I always will be

I pray for her and hope that
She'll never die
And if she does I know she will
Watch me from the sky

Yansan Agard

Mother to Son

Well, son, I'll tell you
Life for me ain't been no crystal stair.
It's had tacks in it,
And splinters,
And boards torn up,
And places with no carpet on the floor –
Bare.
But all the time
I'se been a-climbin' on,
And reachin' landin's,
And turnin' corners,
And sometimes goin' in the dark
Where there ain't been no light.
So, boy, don't you turn back.
Don't you set down on the steps
'Cause you find it kinder hard.
Don't you fall now –
For I'se still goin', honey,
I'se still climbin',
And life for me ain't been no crystal stair.

Langston Hughes

Too Many Daves

Did I ever tell you that Mrs McCave
Had twenty-three sons and she named them all Dave?
Well, she did. And that wasn't a smart thing to do.
You see, when she wants one and calls out, 'Yoo-Hoo!
Come into the house, Dave!' she doesn't get one.
All twenty-three Daves of hers come on the run!
This makes things quite difficult at the McCaves'
As you can imagine, with so many Daves.
And often she wishes that, when they were born,
She had named one of them Bodkin Van Horn
And one of them Hoos-Foos. And one of them Snimm.
And one of them Hot-Shot. And one Sunny Jim.
And one of them Shadrack. And one of them Blinkey.
And one of them Stuffy. And one of them Stinkey.
Another one Putt-Putt. Another one Moon Face.
Another one Marvin O'Gravel Balloon Face.
And one of them Ziggy. And one Soggy Muff.
One Buffalo Bill. And one Biffalo Buff.
And one of them Sneepy. And one Weepy Weed.
And one Paris Garters. And one Harris Tweed.
And one of them Sir Michael Carmichael Zutt
And one of them Oliver Boliver Butt
And one of them Zanzibar Buck-Buck McFate . . .
But she didn't do it. And now it's too late.

Dr Seuss (Theodore Geisel)

Water Everywhere

There's water on the ceiling,
And water on the wall,
There's water in the bedroom,
And water in the hall,
There's water on the landing,
And water on the stair,
Whenever Daddy takes a bath
There's water everywhere.

Valerie Bloom

My Little Sister

My little sister
Likes to eat.
But when she does
She's not too neat.
The trouble is
She doesn't know
Exactly where
The food should go!

William Wise

The Little Boy and the Old Man

Said the little boy, 'Sometimes I drop my spoon.'
Said the little old man, 'I do that too.'
The little boy whispered, 'I wet my pants.'
'I do that too,' laughed the little old man.
Said the little boy, 'I often cry.'
The old man nodded, 'So do I.'
'But worst of all,' said the boy, 'it seems
Grown-ups don't pay attention to me.'
And he felt the warmth of a wrinkled old hand.
'I know what you mean,' said the little old man.

Shel Silverstein

Granny Granny Please Comb My Hair

Granny Granny
please comb my hair
you always take your time
you always take such care

You put me to sit on a cushion
between your knees,
you rub a little coconut oil
parting gentle as a breeze

Mummy Mummy
she's always in a hurry-hurry
rush
she always pulls my hair
sometimes she tugs

But Granny
you have all the time in the world
and when you're finished
you always turn my head and say
'Now who's a nice girl?'

Grace Nichols

Accident!

When I knocked a plate off the table
And it shattered on the floor
And the food spattered over the wall
Dad raised the roof with a roar
'For goodness sake! Be careful!
I've told you so before!'

When dad knocked a mug off the table
And tipped it over the chair
And the coffee spattered across the wall
Dad growled like a grizzly bear
'For goodness sake!' he shook his head
'Who left the coffee there?'

Gervase Phinn

Watch Your French

When my mum tipped a panful of red-hot fat
Over her foot, she did quite a little chat,
And I won't tell you what she said
But it wasn't:
'Fancy that!
I must try in future to be far more careful
With this red-hot scalding fat!'

When my dad fell over and landed – splat! –
With a trayful of drinks (he'd tripped over the cat)
I won't tell you what he said
But it wasn't:
'Fancy that!
I must try in the future to be far more careful
To step *round* our splendid cat!'

When Uncle Joe brought me a cowboy hat
Back from the States, the dog stomped it flat,
And I won't tell you what I said
But Mum and Dad yelled:
'STOP THAT!
Where did you learn that appalling language?
Come on. Where?'

'I've no idea,' I said,
'No idea.'

Kit Wright

PEAS AND HONEY

There is nothing quite as fascinating as food if you're
a baby or toddler, and one could argue that the fascination
does not decrease with age (unlike our waistlines,
unfortunately . . .). Even the saintly Christina Rossetti gets
stuck into the homely ritual of making a pancake, while
Spike Milligan celebrates the sound of eating in a
symphony of slurping ('gobble gobble glup glup').

For any parents maddened by their children's pickiness
about food here is a poem guaranteed to frighten fussy
eaters in the terrifying 'Story of Augustus Who Would Not
Have Any Soup'. Presumably Augustus's parents lived in
the era where if you didn't finish off your plate, it was
brought to you again at the next meal. I always shudder at
those apocryphal stories of children sitting for days in front
of plates of cold tripe . . . I love the incomparable Jack
Prelutsky's 'Chocolate-Covered Salami' because of the way
it summons up the nice (chocolate!) and the nasty (choco-
late fish fricassee!) in such vivid detail, although I wouldn't
recommend trying any of the recipes with your little ones.
Roy Fuller's 'Horrible Things' is another poem exploring the
yuck factor with gruesome relish. Finally, 'Peach' by Rose
Rauter describes so well the sensation of biting into a peach
that it is almost like experiencing it for the first time.

A Thousand Hairy Savages

A thousand hairy savages
Sitting down to lunch
Gobble gobble glup glup
Munch munch munch

Spike Milligan

I Eat My Peas with Honey

I eat my peas with honey;
I've done it all my life.
It makes the peas taste funny,
But it keeps them on the knife.

Anonymous

I Raised a Great Hullabaloo

I raised a great hullabaloo
When I found a large mouse in my stew,
Said the waiter, 'Don't shout
And wave it about,
Or the rest will be wanting one, too!'

Anonymous

Egg Thoughts

Soft-Boiled
I do not like the way you slide,
I do not like your soft inside,
I do not like you many ways,
And I could do for many days
Without a soft-boiled egg.

Sunny-Side-Up
With their yolks and whites all runny
They are looking at me funny.

Sunny-Side-Down
Lying face-down on the plate
On their stomachs there they wait.

Poached
Poached eggs on toast, why do you shiver
With such a funny little quiver?

Scrambled
I eat as well as I am able,
But some falls underneath the table.

Hard-Boiled
With so much suffering today
Why do them any other way?

Russell Hoban

The Pancake

Mix a pancake,
Stir a pancake,
Pop it in the pan.

Fry the pancake,
Toss the pancake,
Catch it if you can.

Christina Rossetti

The Story of Augustus Who Would Not Have Any Soup

Augustus was a chubby lad;
Fat, ruddy cheeks Augustus had;
And everybody saw with joy
The plump and hearty, healthy boy.
He ate and drank as he was told,
And never let his soup grow cold.
But one day, one cold winter's day,
He screamed out – 'Take the soup away!
Oh, take the nasty soup away!
I won't have any soup to-day.'

Next day begins his tale of woes,
Quite lank and lean Augustus grows.
Yet though he feels so weak and ill,
The naughty fellow cries out still –
'Not any soup for me, I say :
Oh, take the nasty soup away!
I won't have any soup to-day.'

The third day comes: oh, what a sin,
To make himself so pale and thin!
Yet, when the soup is put on table,
He screams as loud as he is able –
'Not any soup for me, I say:
Oh, take the nasty soup away!
I won't have any soup to-day.'

Look at him, now the fourth day's come!
He scarcely weighs a sugar plum;
He's like a bit of thread,
And on the fifth day, he was – dead!

Dr Heinrich Hoffmann

Horrible Things

'What's the horriblest thing you've seen?'
Said Nell to Jean.
'Some grey-coloured, trodden on plasticene;
On a plate, a left over cold baked bean;
A cloak-room ticket numbered thirteen;
A slice of meat without any lean;
The smile of a spiteful fairy-tale queen;
A thing in the sea like a brown submarine;
A cheese fur-coated in brilliant green;
A bluebottle perched on a piece of sardine;
What's the horriblest thing *you've* seen?'
Said Jean to Nell.

'Your face, as you tell
Of all the horriblest things you've seen.'

Roy Fuller

I Ate a Tooth This Morning

I ate a tooth this morning,
it was an accident.
It popped into my cereal,
and bingo, down it went.
Before I started breakfast,
that tooth was in my head,
but now that I have swallowed it,
it's somewhere else instead.

It mingled with some raisins,
and landed deep inside.
Perhaps I might have stopped it . . .
I never even tried.
I'm sorry that it happened,
and sorrier to say
that I will never see again
that tooth I ate today.

Jack Prelutsky

Chocolate-Covered Salami

Chocolate-covered salami,
broccoli chocolate fudge,
spinach in chocolate syrup
chocolate sauerkraut sludge.

Pickles in chocolate pudding,
chocolate fish fricassee –
if it has chocolate on it,
it is a snack made for me.

Jack Prelutsky

Peach

Touch it to your cheek and it's soft
as a velvet newborn mouse
who has to strive
to be alive.
Bite in, runny
honey
blooms on your tongue –
as if you've bitten open
a whole hive.

Rose Rauter

THE ENCHANTED KINGDOM

This section is for tales of adventure and magic sure to appeal to escapists young and old. I don't like fairy tales without an element of danger and so I have included Heinrich Heine's story of the magical Loreley. Lore was a mermaid or siren, a beautiful maiden who lived on a rock (the Lei or Ley) on a very dangerous stretch of the river Rhine in Germany. There are various versions of her story: one has it that she was a girl who flung herself into the river in despair over a faithless lover and was transformed into a siren. The Loreley would appear sitting on the rock combing her golden hair and boatmen, enchanted by her beauty and the sound of her singing, would lose control of their boats and drown. This poem has been set to music.

'Overheard on a Saltmarsh' was one of my sister's favourite poems as a child – she liked the strange dialogue between the greedy goblin and the stubborn nymph. The refrains 'Give them me./No' stay in the mind long after you read the poem. 'The Adventures of Isabel' by Ogden Nash was contributed by a friend of my daughter Lydia, and shows the doughty little heroine contending with a bear, witch, giant and (probably worst of all) a doctor. Ogden Nash had two daughters and I think this poem shows he appreciated the toughness of little girls. Dionne

Brand is a Canadian poet with a Caribbean background and here she celebrates story telling by 'old men of magic' who scare and enchant in equal measure. I hope these poems will have the same effect . . .

I had to include Edith Sitwell's reworked nursery rhyme for its powerful imagery and Leo Aylen's 'Somewhere in the Sky' which reminds us that all the best fairy tales contain a mystery. 'Fair Rosa' is a retelling of the classic Sleeping Beauty tale in a satisfyingly rhythmic way, much more like a song than a story. Finally, the classic 'The Fairies' is another poem that comes alive when it is read aloud. It was one of my grandmother's favourites; every time I hear this poem I feel five years old again.

Overheard on a Saltmarsh

Nymph, nymph, what are your beads?

Green glass, goblin. Why do you stare at them?

Give them me.
No.
Give them me. Give them me.
No.
Then I will howl all night in the reeds,
Lie in the mud and howl for them.

Goblin, why do you love them so?

They are better than stars or water,
Better than voices of winds that sing,
Better than any man's fair daughter,
Your green glass beads on a silver ring.

Hush, I stole them out of the moon.

Give me your beads, I want them.

No.

I will howl in a deep lagoon
For your green glass beads, I love them so.
Give them me. Give them me.
No.

Harold Monro

The Loreley

I cannot tell why this imagined
Despair has fallen on me;
The ghost of an ancient legend
That will not let me be:

The air is cool, and twilight
Flows down the quiet Rhine;
A mountain alone in the high light
Still holds the lingering shine.

The last peak rosily gleaming
Reveals, enthroned in air,
A maiden, lost in dreaming,
Who combs her golden hair.

Combing her hair with a golden
Comb in her rocky bower,
She sings the tune of an olden
Song that has magical power.

The boatman has heard; it has bound him
In the throes of a strange, wild love;
Blind to the reefs that surround him,
He sees but the vision above.

And lo, hungry waters are springing –
The boat and the boatman are gone . . .
Then silence. And this, with her singing,
The Loreley has done.

Heinrich Heine
(Translated by Louis Untermeyer)

The Adventures of Isabel

Isabel met an enormous bear,
Isabel, Isabel didn't care;
The bear was hungry, the bear was ravenous,
The bear's big mouth was cruel and cavernous.
The bear said, Isabel, nice to meet you,
How do, Isabel, now I'll eat you!
Isabel, Isabel, didn't worry,
Isabel didn't scream or scurry.
She washed her hands and she straightened her hair up,
Then Isabel quietly ate the bear up.

Once in a night as black as pitch,
Isabel met a wicked old witch.
The witch's face was cross and wrinkled,
The witch's gums with teeth were sprinkled.
Ho ho, Isabel! the old witch crowed,
I'll turn you into an ugly toad,
Isabel, Isabel, didn't worry,
Isabel didn't scream or scurry.
She showed no rage and she showed no rancour,
But she turned the witch into milk and drank her.

Isabel met a hideous giant,
Isabel continued self-reliant.
The giant was hairy, the giant was horrid,
He had one eye in the middle of his forehead.
Good morning, Isabel, the giant said,
I'll grind your bones to make my bread.

Isabel, Isabel, didn't worry.
Isabel didn't scream or scurry.
She nibbled the zwieback that she always fed off,
And when it was gone, she cut the giant's head off.

Isabel met a troublesome doctor,
He punched and he poked till he really shocked her.
The doctor's talk was of coughs and chills,
And the doctor's satchel bulged with pills.
The doctor said unto Isabel
Swallow this, it will make you well.
Isabel, Isabel, didn't worry,
Isabel didn't scream or scurry.
She took those pills from the pill concocter
And Isabel calmly cured the doctor.

Ogden Nash

Old Men of Magic

Old men of magic
with beards long and aged,
speak tales on evenings,
tales so entrancing,
we sit and we listen,
to whispery secrets
about the earth and the heavens.
And late at night,
after sundown they speak
of spirits that live
in silk cotton trees,
of frightening shadows
that sneak through the dark,
and bright balls of fire
that fly in night air,
of shapes unimaginable,
we gasp and we gape,
then just as we're scared
old men of magic
wave hands rough and wrinkled
and all trace of fear disappears.

Dionne Brand

I'd Love to be a Fairy's Child

Children born of fairy stock
Never need for shirt or frock,
Never want for food or fire,
Always get their heart's desire:
Jingle pockets full of gold,
Marry when they're seven years old,
Every fairy child may keep
Two strong ponies and ten sheep;
All have houses, each his own,
Built of brick or granite stone;
They live on cherries, they run wild –
I'd love to be a fairy's child.

Robert Graves

The King of China's Daughter

The King of China's daughter,
So beautiful to see
With her face like yellow water, left
Her nutmeg tree.
Her little rope for skipping
She kissed and gave it me –
Made of painted notes of singing-birds
Among the fields of tea.
I skipped across the nutmeg grove,
I skipped across the sea;
But neither sun nor moon, my dear,
Has yet caught me.

Edith Sitwell

Somewhere in the Sky

Somewhere
In the sky,
There's a door painted blue,
With a big brass knocker seven feet high.
If you can find it,
Knock, and go through –
That is, if you dare.
You'll see behind it
The secrets of the universe piled on a chair
Like a tangle of wool.
A voice will declare
'You have seven centuries in which to unwind it.
But whatever
You do,
You must never,
Ever,
Lose your temper and pull.'

Leo Aylen

Fair Rosa

Fair Rosa was a lovely child
a lovely child a lovely child
fair Rosa was a lovely child
a long time ago

a wicked fairy cast a spell
cast a spell cast a spell
a wicked fairy cast a spell
a long time ago

fair Rosa slept for a hundred years
a hundred years a hundred years
fair Rosa slept for a hundred years
a long time ago

the hedges they all grew around
grew around grew around
the hedges they all grew around
a long time ago

a handsome prince came ariding by
riding by riding by
a handsome prince came ariding by
a long time ago

he cut the hedges one by one
one by one one by one
he cut the hedges one by one
a long time ago

he kissed fair Rosa's lilywhite hand
lilywhite hand lilywhite hand
he kissed fair Rosa's lilywhite hand
a long time ago

fair Rosa will not sleep no more
sleep no more sleep no more
fair Rosa will not sleep no more
a long time ago

Anonymous

The Fairies

Up the airy mountain,
Down the rushy glen,
We daren't go a-hunting
For fear of little men;
Wee folk, good folk,
Trooping all together;
Green jacket, red cap,
And white owl's feather!

Down along the rocky shore
Some make their home –
They live on crispy pancakes
Of yellow tide-foam;
Some in the reeds
Of the black mountain lake,
With frogs for their watch-dogs,
All night awake.

By the craggy hillside,
Through the mosses bare,
They have planted thorn-trees
For pleasure here and there.
Is any man so daring
As dig one up in spite,
He shall find their sharpest thorns
In his bed at night.

Up the airy mountain,
Down the rushy glen,
We daren't go a-hunting
For fear of little men;
Wee folk, good folk,
Trooping all together;
Green jacket, red cap,
And white owl's feather!

William Allingham

A Small Dragon

I've found a small dragon in the woodshed.
Think it must have come from deep inside a forest
because it's damp and green and leaves
are still reflecting in its eyes.

I fed it on many things, tried grass,
the roots of stars, hazel-nut and dandelion,
but it stared up at me as if to say, I need
foods you can't provide.

It made a nest among the coal,
not unlike a bird's but larger,
it is out of place here
and is quite silent.

If you believed in it I would come
hurrying to your house to let you share my wonder,
but I want instead to see
if you yourself will pass this way.

Brian Patten

TOPS TO BOTTOMS

Children love to laugh at the unmentionable (we've all seen them rolling around at fart jokes) and so, even though it's rude to make personal remarks, I had to have some poems about smells, bottoms and dirty faces. 'Miss Nancy Knockabout' is the story of a little girl who wouldn't wash her face while 'Smelly People' deals with the tricky question of body odour. Of course, we all think we smell nicer than everyone else . . . I feel sorry for Mum in this poem who is fingered for smelling of garlic and cabbage! 'Things I Have Been Doing Lately' by Allan Ahlberg is a poem that takes us right inside a ten-year-old, scabs, secrets and all. 'Bottoms' is an amusing poem with a lot of wordplay (something all children love, in common with Shakespeare and crossword puzzle enthusiasts).

'Haircut' is about another rite of passage (who hasn't had a dodgy, parent-inflicted haircut? And had to have everyone notice it?). And of course there had to be a poem about losing teeth – it's funny that this recurs as an anxiety dream in later life because for children the whole process is really rather fun, and of course followed swiftly by a visit from the Tooth Fairy.

Miss Nancy Knockabout

Miss Nancy Knockabout
Wouldn't wash her face
And everybody said
She was a real disgrace.

Mud, soot and marmalade
Smeared across her cheeks and chin
And no-one would think
She had pretty white skin.

Till one day a chimney sweep
Knocked on Nancy's door
And said to Nancy,
'You're the one I adore.'

'Pray won't you marry me?
Your face is just like mine,
We'll be a pair of chimney sweeps,
Won't that be fine.'

But Miss Nancy Knockabout
Screamed and ran away
And ordered twenty pounds of soap
That very same day.

Anonymous

Smelly People

Uncle Oswald smells of tobacco.
Aunt Agatha smells of rope.
Cousin Darren smells of aeroplane glue.
Cousin Tracey smells of soap.

My mum smells of garlic and cabbage.
My dad smells of cups of tea.
My baby sister smells of sick
And my brother of TCP.

Our classroom smells of stinky socks.
Our teacher smells of Old Spice.
I wonder what I smell of?
I'll just have a sniff . . .
hmmm . . . quite nice.

Roger Stevens

Bottoms

Who called a bottom a bottom?
It's not at the bottom at all.
Bottoms are not where our feet are
So bottoms are not what they're called.

I'd call a bottom a middle
It's not at the bottom or top
It's just at the back of the front
The bit where our legs start to stop.

Now feet, they *are* at the bottom
The bottom of me and of you
But think of the problems we'd have
If bottoms were things wearing shoes.

''Scuse me, you stood on my bottom'
'I must rest my bottoms awhile'
Football would hardly be mentioned
As bottomball came into style.

All day we'd stand on our bottoms
Or sit on our middles at school
Someone would stick a bottom out
And cause us to stumble and fall.

But feet don't want to be bottoms
They think they are silly and thick
Which is why whenever they meet
The foot gives the bottom a kick.

Anonymous

Things I Have Been Doing Lately

Things I have been doing lately:
Pretending to go mad
Eating my own cheeks from the inside
Growing taller
Keeping a secret
Keeping a worm in a jar
Keeping a good dream going
Picking a scab on my elbow
Rolling the cat up in a rug
Blowing bubbles in my spit
Making myself dizzy
Holding my breath
Pressing my eyeballs so that I become temporarily blind
Being very nearly ten
Practising my signature . . .

Saving the best till last.

Allan Ahlberg

Haircut

I hate having my hair cut;
And when it's done,
I hate going to school next day
And being *told* about it –
By everyone.

'Oh, you've had your hair cut,' they say.
'Oh, you should wear a hat!'
'Oh, you've had a *bare*-cut,' they say.
And silly things like that.

I can stand having my hair cut,
Though I'd rather let it grow.
What I can't stand
Is being *told* I've had it cut –
As if I didn't know!

Allan Ahlberg

The Tooth Expert

My thithter lotht a tooth today,
I with it had been me,
But I've lotht theven anyway,
You probably can thee,
I love the trickths that you can play,
Beneath a wobbly tooth;
I think I found one yethterday,
Which may be coming looth,
You slide your tongue beneath the gap,
It'th jagged like a thaw,
And if you puth it back and forth,
You loothen it thome more,
But if your tooth is thtubborn,
And thtill hanging by a thread,
You get thome thtring and tie
It to a bed,
Then thomeone hath to tickle you,
And make you jump about,
And tho before you notith the tooth is pulled
Right out!

Susan Stranks

SCHOOL DAZE

School is such a funny place. I once appeared in a documentary about a school I attended, Westminster, and people who know me still remember it because (aged sixteen) I perched on my teacher's desk to talk to him. Nowadays, a pupil sitting on their desk would be the least of a teacher's problems.

'Louder' by Roger Stevens is a hilarious poem about one of those rites of passage we all have to go through, the school concert. There's nothing like over-direction to make the youthful performer wilt . . . 'Sick' by Shel Silverstein commemorates that old trick, throwing a sickie (often still a standby in adult life, if absenteeism rates are anything to go by). 'At the End of School Assembly' is a lovely bit of wordplay which is bound to raise a laugh. 'Odd Girls' by John Coldwell is a very surreal take on the feeling of isolation you can sometimes get when you feel a bit . . . different.

Bullying is such a perennial problem in schools and I thought Roger McGough's poem 'The Boy with the Similar Name' is a very powerful poem because it looks into the mind of the bully, and the fear that lurks there. If you choose a victim perhaps it saves you from being the victim yourself – but, as Roger McGough points out, the shame stays with you all your life. 'Maths' is about a subject where many children must agree with child poet Marjory Fleming: 'I am now going to tell you the horrible and wretched plaege that my multiplication table gives me; you cant conceive it. The most Devilish thing is 8 times 8 and 7 times 7; it is what nature itself cant endure.' I've included some poems about teachers in honour of all teachers everywhere and particularly my friend Emma, and finally 'The Painting Lesson' as a salutary reminder to all grown ups that we don't always know best.

I Don't Want to Go into School

I don't want to go into school today, Mum,
I don't feel like schoolwork today.
Oh, don't make me go into school today, Mum,
Oh, please let me stay home and play.

But you must go to school, my cherub, my lamb.
If you don't it will be a disaster.
How would they manage without you, my sweet,
After all, you are the headmaster!

Colin McNaughton

Teacher

Loud shouter
Deep thinker
Rain hater
Coffee drinker

Spell checker
Sum ticker
Line giver
Nit picker

Ready listener
Trouble carer
Hometime lover
Knowledge sharer

Paul Cookson

Playgrounds

Playgrounds are such gobby places.
Know what I mean?
Everyone seems to have something to
Talk about, giggle, whisper, scream and shout about,
I mean, it's like being in a parrot cage.

And playgrounds are such pushy places.
Know what I mean?
Everyone seems to have to
Run about, jump, kick, do cartwheels, handstands, fly around,
I mean, it's like being inside a whirlwind.

And playgrounds are such patchy places.
Know what I mean?
Everyone seems to
Go round in circles, lines and triangles, coloured shapes,
I mean, it's like being in a kaleidoscope.

And playgrounds are such pally places.
Know what I mean?
Everyone seems to
Have best friends, secrets, link arms, be in gangs.
Everyone, except me.

Know what I mean?

Berlie Doherty

The School Nurse

We're lining up to see the nurse
And in my opinion there's nothing worse.
It is the thing I always dread.
Supposing I've got *nits* in my head.

I go inside and sit on the chair.
She ruffles her fingers in my hair.
I feel my face getting hot and red.
Supposing she finds *nits* in my head.

It's taking ages; it must be bad.
Oh, how shall I tell my mum and dad?
I'd rather see the dentist instead
Than be the one with *nits* in his head.

Then she taps my arm and says, 'Next please!'
And I'm out in the corridor's cooling breeze.
Yet still I can feel that sense of dread.
Supposing she *had* found nits in my head.

Allan Ahlberg

Back to School

In the last week of the holidays
I was feeling glum.
I could hardly wait for school to start;
Neither could mum.

Now we've been back a week,
I could do with a breather.
I can hardly wait for the holidays;
Teacher can't either.

Allan Ahlberg

Teddy Goes to School

'I'm glad to be going to school today'
Said Teddy hearing the bell.
'I am going to learn to read and write
And add and subtract as well.'

'I want to know where Australia is
And where do bananas grow.
I want to know what Eskimoes eat
And why they have all that snow.'

'I want to know where the rivers begin
And what makes the ocean swell,
And how does the salt get in the sea
I know the teachers will tell.'

'I want to know about this big world
And why it's round like a ball,
And I want to know all about giraffes
And what makes their necks so tall.'

'I want to know why birds build their nests up high
And what makes the flowers grow,
And why big aeroplanes can fly so fast
But snails are very slow.'

'I want to know how butterflies are made
And what makes a cricket sing,
I want to be able to spell big words
And how to become a king.'

'I want to know how elephants trumpet
And all about the big whales,
I want to read lots of exciting books
Full of most wonderful tales.'

'I want to know why the sun is so bright
And what makes the church bells ring.
I'm glad I'm going to school today
I want to know everything.'

Brian Miles

The Painting Lesson

'What's THAT, dear?'
Asked the new teacher.
'It's Mummy,'
I replied.
'But mums aren't green and orange!
You really haven't TRIED.
You don't just paint in SPLODGES;
You're old enough to know
You need to THINK before you work.
Now – have another go.'

She helped me draw two arms and legs,
A face with sickly smile,
A rounded body, dark brown hair,
A hat – and in a while
She stood back, with her face bright pink:
'That's SO much better, don't you think?'

But she turned white
At ten to three
When an orange-green blob
Collected me.

'Hi, Mum!'

Trevor Harvey

Louder

OK, Andrew, nice and clearly — off you go.

Welcome everybody to our school concert . . .

Louder, please, Andrew. Mums and dads won't hear you at
The back, will they?

Welcome everybody to our school concert.

Louder, Andrew. You're not trying.
Pro – ject – your – voice.
Take a b i g   b r e a t h and louder!

Welcome everybody to our school concert . . .

For goodness' sake, Andrew. LOUDER! LOUDER!

Welcome every

body to our
school concert!

Now, Andrew, there's no need to be silly.

Roger Stevens

Sick

'I cannot go to school today'
Said little Peggy Ann Mckay.
'I have the measles and the mumps,
A gash, a rash and purple bumps.
My mouth is wet, my throat is dry,
I'm going blind in my right eye.
My tonsils are as big as rocks,
I've counted sixteen chickenpox
And there's one more – that's seventeen,
And don't you think my face looks green?
My leg is cut, my eyes are blue –
It might be instamatic flu.
I cough and sneeze and gasp and choke
I'm sure that my left leg is broke –
My hip hurts when I move my chin,
My belly button's caving in
My back is wrenched, my ankle's sprained,
My 'pendix pains each time it rains.
My nose is cold, my toes are numb,
I have a sliver in my thumb.
My neck is stiff, my voice is weak,
I hardly whisper when I speak.
My tongue is filling up my mouth,
I think my hair is falling out.
My elbow's bent, my spine ain't straight,
My temperature is one-o-eight.
My brain is shrunk, I cannot hear,
There is a hole inside my ear.

I have a hangnail, and my heart is – what?
What's that? What's that you say?
You say today is . . . Saturday
G'bye, I'm going out to play.

Shel Silverstein

At the End of School Assembly

Miss Sparrow's lot flew out,
Mrs Steed's lot galloped out,
Mr Bull's lot herded out,
Mrs Brumble's lot buzzed out.

Miss Rose's class . . . rose,
Mr Beetle's class . . . beetled off,
Miss Storm's class thundered out,
Mrs Frisby's class whirled across the floor.

Mr Train's lot made tracks,
Miss Ferry's lot sailed out,
Mr Roller's got their skates on,
Mrs Street's lot got stuck halfway across the hall.

Mr Idle's class just couldn't be bothered,
Mrs Barrow's class were wheeled out,
Miss Stretcher's class were carried out
And
Mrs Brook's class
Simply
Trickled
Away.

Simon Pitt

Odd Girls

There are some odd girls in our class.
Like Sue whose head is made of glass.
She hangs around with Mary Minns
Whose head is built from baked bean tins.

Now, her best friend is Joanne Green
Whose head is made from plasticine.
And next to her sits Zara Good
Whose head is made from polished wood.
On the desk behind is Cathy Daw
Whose head is made from a bin bag stuffed with straw.
She is pals with Lucy Moon
And her head is a balloon.
At the back sits Tracey Pock
Whose head is just a lump of rock.

They think that I am strange
And leave me all alone.
Is it just because my head
Is made from flesh and bone?

John Coldwell

The Boy with the Similar Name

When Raymond Gough joined our class
He was almost a year behind.
'Sanatorium,' said Mrs McBride
'So I want you all to be kind.'

'Roger, your names are similar
So let Raymond sit next to you.
He'll need a friend to teach him the ropes
And show him what to do.'

Then Teacher went back to teaching
And we went back to being taught
And I tried to be kind to Raymond
But it was harder than I thought.

For he was the colour of candlewax
And smelled of Dettol and Vick.
He was as thin as a sharpened pencil
And his glasses were milk-bottle thick.

Not only that but unfriendly
All muffled up in his shell.
Hobbies? Interests? Ambitions?
It was impossible to tell.

I was afraid of catching his yellowness
And smelling of second-hand Vick
And the only time I could be myself
Were the days when he was off sick.

But what proved to be contagious
Was his oddness, and I knew
That he was a victim ripe for bullying
And so by proxy, I was too.

'How's your brother Raymond?'
The class began to tease,
'Do you share his dirty handkerchiefs?
Do you catch each other's fleas?'

'He's not my brother,' I shouted,
My cheeks all burning hot,
'He's a drippy four eyed monster,
And he comes from the planet Snot.'

They laughed and I saw an opening
(Wouldn't you have done the same?)
I pointed a finger at Raymond
And joined in the bullying game

He stopped coming to school soon after.
'Sanatorium,' said Mrs McBride
He never came back and nobody knew
If he moved elsewhere or died.

I don't think of him very often
For when I do I blush with shame
The thought of the pain I helped inflict
On the boy with the similar name.

Roger McGough

Maths

What do you minus,
and from where?
I ask my teacher,
but he don't care.

Ten cubic metres
in square roots,
Or how many toes
go in nine boots?

Change ten decimals
to a fraction
Aaaaaaaaaahhhhhhhhhh!
is my reaction.

Deepak Kalha

LOOK AROUND YOU . . .

Nature and its cycles are such a source of excitement and wonder when you are young. I'm sure everyone reading this has their own favourite memory: watching the sun come up very early; building your first snowman; jumping in puddles; Bonfire Night . . . I could go on and on. I love Samuel Taylor Coleridge's 'Trees' which, like his 'Answer to a Child's Question', shows an understanding and love of children (he had two sons and one daughter).

The Henry Wadsworth Longfellow and Walter de la Mare poems are both responses to the magic of snow. The 'Calendar Rhyme' by Flora Willis Watson is helpful for remembering the months and seasons while Christina Rossetti's poems about rainbows and the wind are direct, delicate and have a strong emotional appeal (the little girl who contributed 'The Rainbow' read it every night to help her sleep). Finally Roger McGough's 'The Snowman' is an unmissable comic story with a (sniff) surprise ending.

The Snowman

Mother, while you were at the shops
and I was snoozing in my chair
I heard a tap at the window
saw a snowman standing there

He looked so cold and miserable
I almost could have cried
so I put the kettle on
and invited him inside

I made him a cup of cocoa
to warm the cockles of his nose
then he snuggled in front of the fire
for a cosy little doze

He lay there warm and smiling
softly counting sheep
I eavesdropped for a little while
then I too fell asleep

Seems he woke and tiptoed out
exactly when I'm not too sure
it's a wonder you didn't see him
as you came in through the door

(oh, and by the way,
the kitten's made a puddle on the floor)

Roger McGough

The Rainbow

Boats sail on the rivers,
And ships sail on the seas;
But clouds that sail across the sky
Are far prettier than these.

There are bridges on the river,
As pretty as you please;
But the bow that bridges heaven,
And overtops the trees,
And builds a road from earth to sky,
Is far prettier than these.

Christina Rossetti

Wind

I pulled a hummingbird out of the sky one day
    but let it go,
I heard a song and carried it with me
    on my cotton streamers,
I dropped it on an ocean and lifted up a wave
    with my bare hands,
I made a whole canefield tremble and bend
    as I ran by,
I pushed a soft cloud from here to there,
I hurried a stream along a pebbled path,
I scooped up a yard of dirt and hurled it in the air,
I lifted a straw hat and sent it flying,
I broke a limb from a guava tree,
I became a breeze, bored and tired,
And hovered and hung and rustled and lay
    where I could.

Dionne Brand

Roses

You love the roses – so do I. I wish
The sky would rain down roses, as they rain
From off the shaken bush. Why will it not?
Then all the valley would be pink and white
And soft to tread on. They would fall as light
As feathers, smelling sweet: and it would be
Like sleeping and yet waking, all at once.

George Eliot

Calendar Rhyme

January falls the snow,
February cold winds blow,
In March peep out the early flowers,
And April comes with sunny showers.
In May the roses bloom so gay,
In June the farmer mows his hay,
In July brightly shines the sun,
In August harvest is begun.
September turns the green leaves brown,
October winds then shake them down,
November fills with bleak and smear,
December comes and ends the year.

Flora Willis Watson

Night

The sun descending in the west,
The evening star does shine,
The birds are silent in their nest,
And I must seek for mine.
The moon, like a flower
In heaven's high bower,
With silent delight
Sits and smiles on the night.

William Blake

The Early Morning

The moon on the one hand, the dawn on the other:
The moon is my sister, the dawn is my brother.
The moon on my left and the dawn on my right.
My brother, good morning: my sister, good night.

Hilaire Belloc

Wet

Wet wet wet
the world of melting winter,
icicles weeping themselves away
on the eaves
little brown rivers streaming
down the road
nibbling
at the edges of the tired snow,
   all puddled mud
   not a dry place to put
   a booted foot,
everything
   dripping
   slipping
   gushing
   slushing
and listen to that brook
rushing
like a puppy loosed from its leash.

Lilian Moore

Weather

Whether the weather be fine or whether the weather be not,
Whether the weather be cold, or whether the weather be hot,
We'll weather the weather, whatever the weather,
Whether we like it or not.

Anonymous

Who Has Seen the Wind?

Who has seen the wind?
Neither I nor you:
But when the leaves hang trembling
The wind is passing through.

Who has seen the wind?
Neither you nor I:
But when the trees bow down their heads
The wind is passing by.

Christina Rossetti

Trees

The Oak is called the King of Trees,
The Aspen quivers in the breeze,
The Poplar grows up straight and tall,
The Pear tree spreads along the wall,
The Sycamore gives pleasant shade
The Willow droops in watery glade,
The Fir tree useful timber gives,
The Beech amid the forest lives.

Samuel Taylor Coleridge

Snow

Out of the bosom of the air,
Out of the cloudfolds of her garment shaken,
Over the woodlands, brown and bare,
Over the harvest-fields forsaken
Silent, and soft, and slow
Descends the snow.

Henry Wadsworth Longfellow

The Snowflake

Before I melt,
Come, look at me!
This lovely icy filigree!
Of a great forest
In one night
I make a wilderness
Of white:
By skyey cold
Of crystals made,
All softly, on
Your finger laid,
I pause, that you
My beauty see:
Breathe, and I vanish
Instantly.

Walter de la Mare

If Pigs Could Fly

If pigs could fly, I'd fly a pig
To foreign countries small and big –
To Italy and Spain,
To Austria, where cowbells ring,
To Germany, where people sing –
And then come home again.

I'd see the Ganges and the Nile;
I'd visit Madagascar's isle,
And Persia and Peru.
People would say they'd never seen
So odd, so strange an air-machine
As that on which I flew.

Why, everyone would raise a shout
To see his trotters and his snout
Come floating from the sky;
And I would be a famous star
Well known in countries near and far –
If only pigs could fly!

James Reeves

I'M COMING TO GET YOU . . .

Here are ghoulies, ghosties and things that go bump in the night . . . Not all for the faint of heart, but some children, like my nephew Felix, seem to thrive on these stories (his favourite word is 'scary'). Like many small boys, he is also very fond of dinosaurs, so I've included 'Ode to an Extinct Dinosaur' for all dinomaniacs. 'The Troll' is by the fantastic children's poet Jack Prelutsky, who seems to have a poem for every subject: his troll is genuinely scary, but very funny as well.

A lot of children's poems draw on the macabre for humour and I think 'Father and Mother' by X. J. Kennedy and 'Colonel Fazackerley' by Charles Causley are miniature comic masterpieces. 'The Visitor' on the other hand is genuinely chilling. Definitely not one for late at night. As the child who contributed this poem pointed out, it has a strong moral! Children will love the humour in Spike Milligan's wonderful 'Granny Boot', which tells the tale of a haunted (or at the very least possessed) item of footwear.

Ode to an Extinct Dinosaur

Iguanadon, I loved you,
With all your spiky scales,
Your massive jaws,
Impressive claws
And teeth like horseshoe nails.

Iguanadon, I loved you.
It moved me close to tears
When first I read
That you've been dead
For ninety million years.

Doug MacLeod

The Hag

The hag is astride,
This night for to ride –
The devil and she together;
Through thick and through thin,
Now out and then in,
Though ne'er so foul be the weather.

A thorn or a burr
She takes for a spur;
With a lash of the bramble she rides now
Through brakes and through briers,
O'er ditches and mires,
She follows the spirit that guides now.

No beast, for his food,
Dares now range the wood,
But husht in his lair he lies lurking;
While mischiefs, by these,
On land and on seas,
At noon of night are a-working.

The storm will arise,
And trouble the skies,
This night; and, more the wonder,
The ghost from the tomb
Affrighted shall come,
Called out by the clap of the thunder.

Robert Herrick

The Troll

Be wary of the loathsome troll
that slyly lies in wait
to drag you to his dingy hole
and put you on his plate.

His blood is black and boiling hot,
he gurgles ghastly groans.
He'll cook you in his dinner pot,
your skin, your flesh, your bones.

He'll catch your arms and clutch your legs
and grind you to a pulp,
then swallow you like scrambled eggs –
gobble! gobble! gulp!

So watch your steps when next you go
upon a pleasant stroll,
or you might end up in the pit below
as supper for the troll.

Jack Prelutsky

Father and Mother

My father's name is Frankenstein,
He comes from the Barbados.
He fashioned me from package twine
And instant mashed potatoes.

My mother's name is Draculeen,
She lets a big bat bite her,
And folks who sleep here overnight
Wake up a few quarts lighter.

X. J. Kennedy

Colonel Fazackerley

Colonel Fazackerley Butterworth-Toast
Bought an old castle complete with ghost,
But someone or other forgot to declare
To Colonel Fazack that the spectre was there.

On the very first evening, while waiting to dine,
The Colonel was taking a fine sherry wine,
When the ghost, with a furious flash and a flare,
Shot out of the chimney and shivered 'Beware!'

Colonel Fazackerley put down his glass
And said, 'My dear fellow, that's really first class!
I just can't conceive how you do it at all.
I imagine you're going to a Fancy Dress Ball?'

At this, the dread ghost gave a withering cry.
Said the Colonel (his monocle firm in his eye),
'Now just how you do it I wish I could think.
Do sit down and tell me, and please have a drink.'

The ghost in his phosphorous cloak gave a roar
And floated about between ceiling and floor.
He walked through a wall and returned through a pane
And backed up the chimney and came down again.

Said the Colonel, 'With laughter I'm feeling quite weak!'
(As trickles of merriment ran down his cheek).
'My house-warming party I hope you won't spurn.
You must say you'll come and you'll give us a turn!'

At this, the poor spectre – quite out of his wits –
Proceeded to shake himself almost to bits.
He rattled his chains and he clattered his bones
And he filled the whole castle with mumbles and groans.

But Colonel Fazackerley, just as before,
Was simply delighted and called out, 'Encore!'
At which the ghost vanished, his efforts in vain,
And never was seen at the castle again.

'Oh dear, what a pity!' said Colonel Fazack.
'I don't know his name, so I won't call him back.'
And then with a smile that was hard to define,
Colonel Fazackerley went in to dine.

Charles Causley

The Visitor

A crumbling churchyard, the sea and the moon;
The waves had gouged out grave and bone;
A man was walking late and alone . . .

He saw a skeleton on the ground;
A ring on a bony finger he found.

He ran home to his wife and gave her the ring
'Oh where did you get it?' He said not a thing.

'It's the loveliest ring in the world,' she said
As it glowed on her finger they slipped off to bed.

At midnight they woke. In the dark outside,
'Give me my ring!' a chill voice cried.

'What was that, William? What did it say?'
'Don't worry, my dear. It'll soon go away.'

'I'm coming!' A skeleton opened the door.
'Give me my ring!' It was crossing the floor.

'What was that, William? What did it say?'
'Don't worry my dear, it'll soon go away.'

'I'm reaching you now! I'm climbing the bed.'
The wife pulled the sheet right over her head.

It was torn from her grasp and tossed in the air.
'I'll drag you out of bed by the hair!'

'What was that, William? What did it say?'
'Throw the ring through the window, THROW IT AWAY!'

She threw it. The skeleton leapt from the sill,
Scooped up the ring and clattered downhill.
Fainter . . . and fainter . . . then all was still.

Ian Serraillier

Granny Boot

Granny in her bed one night
Heard a little squeak!
And then a little
Peck-peck-peck
Like something with a beak
Then something that went Binkle-Bonk
Ickle-tickle-toot
And all of it was coming
From inside Grandma's boot!
Then the boot began to *hop*
It went into the hall
And then from deep inside the boot
Came a Tarzan call
The sound of roaring lions
The screech of a cockatoo
Today that boot is in a cage
Locked in the London Zoo.

Spike Milligan

DON'T DO AS I DO, DO AS I SAY

'I don't want to . . .' How many times have you heard that cry with a lurch of frustration? Well, Jack Prelutsky's 'I Don't Want To' reminds us all just how it feels when you have a bad case of the blues and nothing, not even a hug, will fix it. The clue perhaps is in the last two lines – it's hard sometimes to know what you want. Carl Sandburg, the famous left-wing American poet, seems an unlikely expert on what kids get up to, but I think 'Why Did the Children' sums up very nicely how children home in on the one activity they are forbidden. Perhaps telling them not to pour molasses on the cat just gave them the idea . . .

'Advice to Children' is just what it says on the bottle, while Henry Wadsworth Longfellow's 'There Was a Little Girl' always makes me smile. I love Karla Kuskin's 'Rules' which makes fun of the silliness of some of the rules we set up for our children, and I'm sure it will strike a chord with any child. Karla Kuskin was an only child who grew up without TV and was a great reader and keen artist all her life: she says her childhood is one of her main inspirations and I think that shows in her poetry. Jack Prelutsky, on the other hand, hated poetry (he thought it was like liver, supposed to be good for you but not actually enjoyable) and it was only when he started writing poetry in his twenties that he realised poetry could be 'delightful' and about subjects children really care about.

I Don't Want To

I don't want to play on the sidewalk.
I don't want to sit on the stoop.
I don't want to lick any ice-cream.
I don't want to slurp any soup.
I don't want to listen to music.
I don't want to look at cartoons.
I don't want to read any stories.
I don't want to blow up balloons.

I don't want to dig in the garden.
I don't want to roll on the rug.
I don't want to wrestle the puppy.
I don't want to give you a hug.
I don't want to shoot any baskets.
I don't want to bang on my drum.
I don't want to line up my soldiers.
I don't want to whistle or hum.

I don't want to program my robot.
I don't want to strum my guitar.
I don't want to use my computer.
I don't want to wind up my car.
I don't want to color with crayons.
I don't want to model with clay.
I don't want to stop my not wanting . . .
I'm having that kind of a day.

Jack Prelutsky

Why Did the Children

'Why did the children
put beans in their ears
when the one thing we told the children
they must not do
was put beans in their ears?'

'Why did the children
pour molasses on the cat
when the one thing we told the children
they must not do
was pour molasses on the cat?'

Carl Sandburg

Advice to Small Children

Eat no green apples or you'll droop,
Be careful not to get the croup,
Avoid the chicken-pox and such,
And don't fall out of windows much.

Edward Anthony

There Was a Little Girl

There was a little girl, who had a little curl
Right in the middle of her forehead,
And when she was good, she was very, very good,
But when she was bad she was horrid.

Henry Wadsworth Longfellow

Going Through the World

As I was running
Up the down escalator
I passed Jeff Nuttall
Running down the up

Tom Pickard

Rules

Do not jump on ancient uncles.
Do not yell at average mice.
Do not wear a broom to breakfast.
Do not ask a snake's advice.
Do not bathe in chocolate pudding.
Do not talk to bearded bears.
Do not smoke cigars on sofas.
Do not dance on velvet chairs.
Do not take a whale to visit
Russell's mother's cousin's yacht.

And whatever else you do
It is better you
Do not.

Karla Kuskin

SHE'S MY BEST FRIEND, I HATE HER!

The title for this chapter comes from a remark I made as a child and have never been allowed to forget! 'I Had an Invisible Playmate' is about an imaginary friend, a childhood staple, although often a lot of work to keep up. Perhaps that's why it ended up getting squashed on the sofa . . . 'I Hate Harry' is about when friends fall out, which, let's face it, is one of the defining experiences of childhood. At least the arguments don't always last that long, even when the feelings are as strong as they are in this poem! Friendship is a complicated emotion when you are young and don't have jobs, cars or trophy wives or husbands to establish your place in the playground pecking order. 'Puzzle' gives a good take on the trickiness of childhood friendships.

I put 'I Saw a Little Girl I Hate' in because it made me laugh; I think it shows how tricky male–female friendships can be even before we hit our teens! And finally, I've put Emily Brontë's 'Love is like the wild rose-briar' in because it makes the point that friendship is still a lot more enduring than love. I have friendships that have endured over decades and that's a hard thing to say, sadly, about most love affairs.

I Had an Invisible Playmate

I had an invisible playmate
that nobody else seemed to see,
I doubt they believed it existed,
it showed itself only to me.
Sometimes we chased one another,
sometimes we went for a walk,
sometimes we sat down together
and had a good heart-to-heart talk.

We tossed an invisible beach ball,
we jumped an invisible rope,
we planted invisible flowers,
we climbed an invisible slope.
I thought we'd be playmates forever,
but everything comes to an end –
my grandmother sat on the sofa,
and squashed my invisible friend.

Jack Prelutsky

I Hate Harry

I hate Harry like . . . like . . . OOO!
I hate Harry like . . . GEE!
I hate that Harry like – poison.
I hate! hate! hate! HAR – RY!

Rat! Dope! Skunk! Bum! Liar!
Dumber than the dumbest dumb flea!
BOY! . . . do I hate Harry,
I hate him the most that can be.

I hate him a hundred, thousand, million
Double, and multiplied by three,
A skillion, trillion zillion more times
Than Harry, that rat, hates me.

Miriam Chaikin

Puzzle

My best friend's name is Billy
But his best friend is Fred
And Fred's is Willy Wiffleson
And Willy's best is Ted.
Ted's best pal is Samuel
While Samuel's is Paul . . .
It's funny Paul says I'm his best
I hate him most of all.

Arnold Spilka

I Saw a Little Girl I Hate

I saw a little girl I hate
And kicked her with my toes.
She turned
And smiled
And KISSED me!
Then she punched me in the nose.

Arnold Spilka

Love is like the wild rose-briar

Love is like the wild rose-briar,
Friendship like the holly-tree
The holly is dark when the rose-briar blooms
But which will bloom most constantly?

The wild rose-briar is sweet in the spring,
Its summer blossoms scent the air;
Yet wait till winter comes again
And who will call the wild-briar fair?

Then scorn the silly rose-wreath now
And deck thee with the holly's sheen
That when December blights the brow
He may still leave thy garland green.

Emily Brontë

TUCKED IN

I remember the sensation of being tucked into bed by my grandmother, and hating it when she turned out the light. I thought there were murderers lurking in the corridor. So many children are afraid of the dark or of monsters in their bedroom. I particularly like The Man in Black who lurks behind the bedroom door, but I think most people can relate to The Hand. Where the narrator says The Hand 'is under there all right' it's very easy to sympathise. Most people have some bedtime quirk, which stays with them all their lives: sleeping with the light on or off, having to close the wardrobe door . . . Well, this is how it starts.

One way to cure the night time terrors is to share with someone, and I particularly love 'In Isas Bed' by the little girl author Marjory Fleming. Throughout her short life she wrote a great deal and several of her poems were about her beloved cousin Isabel who helped with her education and upbringing. The poet wrote in her diary 'I disturbed her repose at night by contunial figiting and kicking but I was very contunialy at work reading the Arabin nights entertainment which I could not have done had I slept at the top'.

We've all had the experience of the peculiarly vivid dream which seems almost more convincing than reality and here is Jack Prelutsky writing about it in 'Last Night I Dreamed of Chickens'. Finally, I love 'Thinking in Bed' by Dennis Lee for its metaphysical speculation and 'Human Affection' by Stevie Smith for its warm appreciation of the love between mother and child.

Bedtime

When I go upstairs to bed,
I usually give a loud cough.
This is to scare the Monster off.

When I come to my room,
I usually slam the door right back.
This is to squash The Man in Black
Who sometimes hides there.

Nor do I walk to the bed,
But usually run and jump instead.
This is to stop The Hand –
Which is under there all right –
From grabbing my ankles.

Allan Ahlberg

In Isas Bed

I love in Isas bed to lie
O such joy and luxury
The bottom of the bed I sleep
And with great care I myself keep
Oft I embrace her feet of lillys
But she has goton all the pillies.
Her neck I never can embrace
But I do hug her feet in place
But I am sure I am contented
And of my follies am repented
I am sure I'd rather be
In a small bed at liberty

Marjory Fleming

Last Night I Dreamed of Chickens

Last night I dreamed of chickens
there were chickens everywhere,
they were standing on my stomach,
they were nesting in my hair,
they were pecking at my pillow,
they were hopping on my head,
they were ruffling up their feathers
as they raced about my bed.

They were on the chairs and tables,
they were on the chandeliers
they were roosting in the corners,
they were clucking in my ears,
there were chickens, chickens, chickens
for as far as I could see . . .
when I woke today, I noticed
there were eggs on top of me.

Jack Prelutsky

There was an Old Man of Moldavia

There was an Old Man of Moldavia,
Who had the most curious behaviour;
    For while he was able,
    He slept on a table
That funny Old Man of Moldavia

Edward Lear

Thinking in Bed

I'm thinking in bed,
Cause I can't get out
Till I learn how to think
What I'm thinking about;
What I'm thinking about
Is a person to be –
A sort of person
Who feels like me.

I might still be Alice,
Excepting I'm not
And Snoopy is super
But not when it's hot;
I couldn't be Piglet
I don't think I'm Pooh,
I know I'm not Daddy
And I can't be you.

My breakfast is waiting.
My clothes are all out,
But what was that thing
I was thinking about?
I'll never get up
If I lie here all day;
But I still haven't thought
So I'll just have to stay.

If I was a Grinch
I expect I would know.
But I don't think so.
There's so many people
I don't seem to be –
I guess I'll just have to
Get up and be me.

Dennis Lee

Bye, Baby Bunting

Bye, baby bunting,
Daddy's gone a-hunting,
Gone to get a rabbit skin
To wrap the baby bunting in.

Anonymous

Human Affection

Mother, I love you so.
Said the child, I love you more than I know.
She laid her head on her mother's arm,
And the love between them kept them warm.

Stevie Smith

ACKNOWLEDGEMENTS

JOHN AGARD: 'Swimming Teeth' from *We Animals Would Like a Word With You* (The Bodley Head, 1996), reprinted by permission of The Random House Group Ltd. ALLAN AHLBERG: 'Things I Have Been Doing Lately' from *Heard It in the Playground* (Viking, 1989), copyright © Allan Ahlberg 1989, 'Haircut', 'The School Nurse', 'Back to School' and 'Bedtime' from *Please Mrs Butler* (Kestrel, 1983), copyright © Allan Ahlberg 1983, reprinted by permission of Penguin Books Ltd. EDWARD ANTHONY: 'Advice to Small Children' from *Every Dog has his Day* (Watson Guphill, 1975). LEO AYLEN: 'Somewhere in the Sky' from *Rhymoceros* (Macmillan Education, 1989), reprinted by permission of the author. HILAIRE BELLOC: 'The Elephant' and 'The Frog' from *The Bad Child's Book of Beasts* (Duckworth, 1903), copyright © The Estate of Hilaire Belloc, and 'Early Morning' from *Sonnets and Verse* (Duckworth, 1923), copyright © The Estate of Hilaire Belloc, reprinted by permission of PFD (www.pfd.co.uk) on behalf of the Estate of Hilaire Belloc VALERIE BLOOM: 'Water Everywhere' from *Let Me Touch the Sky* (Macmillan Children's Books, 2000), copyright © Valerie Bloom 2000, reprinted by permission of Valerie Bloom c/o Eddison Pearson Ltd. DIONNE BRAND: 'Old Men of Magic' and 'Wind' from *Earth Magic* (Kids Can Press, 1979), copyright © Dionne Brand 1979, reprinted by permission of the author and the publishers. WALTER R. BROOKS: 'Ants, Although Admirable Are Awfully Aggravating' from *The Collected Poems of Freddy the Pig* (Alfred A Knopf, 1953). CHARLES CAUSLEY: 'Colonel Fazackerley' from *Figgie Hobbin* (Macmillan Children's Books, 2002), reprinted by permission of David Higham Associates. JOHN COLDWELL: 'Odd Girls', copyright © John Coldwell 2001, first published in *Ridiculous Rhymes* edited by John Foster (HarperCollins, 2001), reprinted by permission of the author. PAUL COOKSON: 'Teacher', first published as 'Mrs Kenning' in *Crazy Classrooms and Secret Staffrooms* (Lion, 2001), reprinted by permission of the author. WALTER DE LA MARE: 'Snowflake' from *The Complete Poems of Walter de la Mare* (Faber, 1969), reprinted by permission of The Literary Trustees of Walter de la Mare and The Society of Authors as their representative. PETER DIXON: 'Magic Cat' from *Peter Dixon's Grand Prix of Poetry* (Macmillan Children's Books, 1999), reprinted by permission of the author. BERLIE DOHERTY: 'Playgrounds' reprinted by permission of David Higham Associates. ROY FULLER: 'Horrible Things' from *The World Through the Window* (Blackie Children's Books, 1989), reprinted by permission of John Fuller. ROBERT GRAVES: 'I'd Love to be a Fairy's Child' from *Complete Poems in One* edited by Beryl Graves and Dunstan Ward (2000), reprinted by permission of the publishers, Carcanet Press Ltd. TREVOR HARVEY: 'The Painting Lesson', copyright © Trevor Harvey 1990, first published in *Funny Poems* edited by Heather Amery (Usborne Books, 1990), reprinted by permission of the author. RUSSELL HOBAN: 'Egg Thoughts' from *Egg Thoughts* (Faber, 1973), reprinted by permission of David Higham Associates. LANGSTON HUGHES: 'Mother to Son' from *The Collected Poems of Langston Hughes* (Alfred A. Knopf, 1994), reprinted by permission of David

INDEX